MELODIES
OF MY OTHER LIFE

VANESSA
MATTHEWS

Winter Goose
Publishing

Winter Goose Publishing
2701 Del Paso Road, 130-92
Sacramento, CA 95835

www.wintergoosepublishing.com
Contact Information: info@wintergoosepublishing.com

Melodies of My Other Life

COPYRIGHT ©2013 by Vanessa Matthews

First Edition, March 2013

Cover Art by Winter Goose Publishing
Photograph by Vanessa Matthews
Typeset by Michelle Lovi

ISBN: 978-0-9889049-7-2

Published in the United States of America

This book is dedicated to who I was,
who I am,
and who I've yet to be

Contents

VOLUME 3 – BITTER BALLADS & HARD BEATS 59

VOLUME 4 – CANTATA OF SELF COMPOSURE

VOLUME 1
SONGS OF SWEET & LIGHT

Cloud Busting

Syrup dew surrounds me with
a swaddle of fresh mown lawn
been lying here since daybreak
staring skyward, pictures drawn

Fluttered shapes regale me
clouds pop by in candy floss
sink back as fairy tales unfold
while vibrant dream scenes toss

They tumble like a circus
perform in sequences unseen
before today in sweet bewilder
misted shapes that twist between

Clouds busting up, breaking down,
rise again to mount their climb
exquisitely imperfect form
nothing normal by design

They recede and then return
sun chases frazzled plumes away
flaunts the petticoats of spring
no better time than start of day

To catch clouds 'tween nimble fingers
sprinkle ten grass-speckled toes
stem ginger traces crystalize on
freckled brow and pixie nose

Slowing the moves of busy bees
racing past and picking petals
sitting tight, on dusted stamen
perfect morning, none unsettled

Never could, or ever would
break the clouds today, too much
making fun just lying here
picking clouds with childish clutch

Grandma Dot's Pearls

The door creaks softly
in I go
tiptoe, tiptoe

Grandma Dot's snoozing
duped by late suns ray

So enticing, inviting me
to stay, linger a while

Cottage flowers spread
on fresh clean linen

I look out again
onto the landing
all clear
tiptoe, tiptoe

Running smooth hands
across threadbare velvet
resist the urge to pick, pull

Settle at the dressing table
bare feet don't touch down
just swing to and fro

Walking my fingers over
brushes, lotions, potions
. . . *all this lady stuff*

Open the drawer and paw
beads, sparkles and pearls
wisdom of years sprinkled
in Yardley's lavender

Peeking in the mirror
too small to see full face
just Celtic lines, rouge tones
appled cheekbones set
beneath curious eyes

The world of womanhood
is a wondrous place indeed
I see myself reflected that way
as I brush thick wavy hair
black as night with a hint of blue
swish and sway it, then let go
watch it fall across soft shoulders

One day soon, and so
tiptoe, tiptoe

Teasing out time's prettiest gems
a kaleidoscope of costume from
the days before Grandma was
betrayed by an inch of grey now primed by the bottle,
though the glint of mischief
remains in her shrinking, twinkling eyes

Surrounded by a blanket of ancestry
Welsh women's blood in vein
aunts and mother
a family heritage that awaits

Until then I go
tiptoe, tiptoe
and keep dancing
in Grandma Dot's pearls

Pantry Days

Shelves to the ceiling
reveal the secrets of first tasted
moments, that melt in the mouth
hundreds and thousands
sprinkled in spun sugar
sweethearts and scones
fizz in my tummy, now fuzzy
with the flavours and perfumes
of the pantry, always open
"Help yourself" would come the call
as I skipped into the kitchen
fingers licked at the possibilities
my second home in her arms
pantry days surrounding me

Of Knights and Shining Armor

Galloping into view
a knight on alabaster charge
come to rescue me
from my rug swamp
or cardboard tower built high
Lay in wait, palm to brow
love's kiss to break a spell
cast to keep me here
in lands awash with daydreams
and battle-won hearts
my favor thrown to the rainbows
Only stepping out of this wonderland
do I see your smile
at the doorway of my reverie
my blushes rise like roses
and I grimace at the thought of
being caught up in tales
of Knights and shining armor

High Life in Homestead

Our street was one of red brick
and hot summer tarmac.

Mirages risen from the sticky black
as we ran with tender feet
door to door, house to house.

The soggy remains of water fights
our battleground sun dried in a quick fix.

Home before dark or woe betide,
kiss chase and scuffles
from spring to autumn term.

Freedom afforded by community,
not under lock and key then.

Heart racing at the taste of independence,
took things on the chin
or wailed your way back home to Mom.

Then wait.

Is that the ice cream man calling a tune?
Just after dinner, how did he know?

One of the mysteries
of high times at Homestead.

Made for Me

The chug along of the sewing machine
would rouse a certain curiosity

To watch you cut and plot, and interlock
wonder what would take shape under the needle

Threads of mix and match coming together
from the Fancy Silk Store in town

We'd delved hand in hand through
the maze of voile, muslin, cotton, brocade
Sari satins, chiffon, and stretched lace
from floor
to floor
to floor
to ceiling, and wall to wall between

Pearlescent, gold, spangled, and sheer
too old for my tiny years so instead
edged with broderie anglaise or
a touch of smocking, gingham cut
on the bias with girlish trim

And that's how it was, made just for me
proudly twirling in love-spun dresses

Taking Tea with Aunt Alice

Snow, rain, or English sunshine, it was inconsequential to Aunt Alice. Our kindly neighbor with a lack of relativity that was not relevant to either of us. Her door was always open to me, offered with a free pass to warmly-wobbled words delivered with delicate wisdom.

Her smile shined from crepe skin as age-spotted hands reached for the kettle. I was just nine years old and she ninety-two, but it mattered little to us and I could spend hours getting lost in her ways. Old puckered lips trembling at the bite of a digestive biscuit. Careful, so as not to disturb her teeth. Tripping out stories in soft warble, she'd tell of the old days as we shared new days. Together. Book ends in many ways. Old souls, her and I. Seeking, sharing, and exchanging our charm until the teapot emptied.

Then the fatigue of her years would wash over her fragile frame pulling her under the afternoon. Sat tight in her chair, facing south through the seasons, that was the time when the garden would call me to explore. Almost an acre of winding lawn stretched out like a finger pointing down toward an opening in the fence, a passageway to the woodland and canal side.

In autumn I would watch leaves fall like feathers floating between the gnarled branches of the giant oak at the center of the plot. A wall of conifers stood proud like soldiers against harsh winter snow. Their resilience never failed to impress me.

In spring and summer the green canvas came back to life. Cherry trees speckled fresh cut grass with a pastel palette. And the bluebells delighted in that magical moment when their buds opened, taking first place in the race against the other woodland flowers. Pinpricks of blue heralding the onset of longer warmer days.

On these days, as Aunt Alice took her nap, I would tiptoe down to the opening in the fence, then meander out to skip through the rich blue carpet of flowers. A blue so vivid it could put the seas and the skies to shame. Almost royal in its hue, I would imagine myself wrapped in it as cloak and gown.

Me the bluebell princess, Aunt Alice my lady in waiting. Her limbs not stiff, her lips not trembling, just dancing her and I, spinning and laughing in daydream until the last day of spring. The story between our book ends stretched until halted by time's passing, the daydream held in the safety of our dancing foot prints.

Meet Me in the Middle

"Grandma?" I asked one Saturday.
"Why don't my hands meet when I hug you around your middle?"
Every time I would be tickled by the challenge of it
and how she'd chuckled
sweet and warm as fresh baked Welsh cakes.
Me too, until our eyes glistened
and she and I, still in hold, would rattle together.
An envelope of love and family ties
cushioned by her dough-like form that offered comforts
like the plumpest of goose-feather duvets.
I had always been just dotty about Grandma.

The Summer of Catalan's Girl

Chocolate eyes steeped in romance,
the face of a Catalan child, they say.
Blue-black waves of hair crash against
alabaster skin, now in olive bloom.

I'd pretend in native tongue; you'd hear,
held dear, in the close evening air.
Senses tickled by flavours of
banyan that sprout from generous host.
That sways and swells with pride,
then sighs at the thought of belonging.

Magic weaves this delighted daughter
a wink and nod, sitting . . . pretty . . . sweet.
Blossoms through heart and sight, as the sea
lays a hammock under pomegranate skies.

Carry me home, close, safe
in sleepy cradle until sunrise brings
sticky heat, and more, more
loveliness, like this.

Buckets and Bubble Gum

Every Friday night straight from school
blankets, pillows, a fishing net, and a faded bucket
all forced into my dad's old Ford, the trunk barely closing

Squashed together on the back seat, happily so
as we headed out for another weekend
of horse riding and card games under cover

Cranking up the car radio as we sang through the hours
Uncle Terry and my dad in cowboy boots rain or shine
my brother and my cousin trying to shake me off on arrival

Bubble gum and penny chews from the store
I swear the sun shone brighter there, the rain felt wetter
even now the sound of rain on a tin roof takes me back

To the days when there was nothing to do but drift away

In the Small of Your Back

I'd sit in the small of your back
plaiting your hair as you lay
tummy to carpet, hands under chin.

We'd watch them twirl, you and I.

Sparkles and chiffon, froth and flair,
toe pick then twist into Triple Salchow,
taking flight, so graceful you said.
Artistic impression. Technical merit.

You'd score, I'd score, and we'd smile.

Run our own commentary in the space
between routines, cupcakes from the pantry
our little treat, and I'd watch in awe
of those figure skaters. And of you.
Ice skating was not for me, nor any sport.

I've always been afraid, you see.

But instinctively, I knew it made you smile
so I tossed and tumbled, elegance free,
my spiral straggling and my sit spin too high.
Not like you, carving ice castles everywhere.

All I could do to glide in your lines, hang on.

Bear witness to the flair and flow,
you brought it to life, with costumes created.
Ribbon trimmed and sequins strewn.
I dressed up, but like a puppy in clown suit,
cute but ridiculous.

You, you lit up every room.

Wore everything as if tailored to suit.
It was just what you did, who you were.
And I'd sit happy there (the small of your back),
hoping someday it might rub off on me.

Evolutionary Girl

Not a revolutionary by any means,
though changing nonetheless,
or, she ponders, a changeling perhaps.
Away with fairies in head and heart,
hand in hand with folklore
believing in the joy of simplicity.

Pleasures found in pear-drop kisses,
sherbet smiles and liquorice.
Invisible friends to the end, and always
with a carefully choreographed dance.
Carrying a hum in her pocket
that sang soft as she imagined
a ladybird might with wings in flutter.

Puzzled at her growing, skin plumped
with new shape showing under slip.
Hint of pout in her lip, diamonds in eyes
revealing her gifts slowly and with poise.
Like Christmas morning without the cold.
Snap! A matching pair in their ways.
Evolutionary, as the girl gives hint
of the woman before them both.

Daddy's Nelly Bean

You're Daddy in my eyes, though at times
they'd say (and I knew it too),
You're the image of your mother.
I was, it's true, but also a glimmer
of you reflected in my face.

Watching you all dirt and soil.
Hard labors, digging deep.
Self-made man in Derry boots,
little splats of mud, bramble cuts,
the scent of peat and hard-earned sweat.

Weathered face beset with a bright smile.
Twinkle in your eye, charming to
the ladies, and her. Your lady.
She was your reason to toil, after all.
And I, sister to a brother who came first,
but me, the apple fell fresh from your tree.
Sat nestled amongst the green,
an island you created for me in a flash
of silver spade and fork,
surrounding me with gifts of you and more.

Stubble-scratched kisses to my nose
as you recreated my world, me at the center
(at least that's how you made me feel)
with one more day of graft.
So I could hop aboard the blue rope swing,
take the thrills of spin and slide.

For her a one-hundred-foot weave of green
to become an acre later,
when roses around the door
of a perfect home would be the dream.
Simple pleasures for a simpler time.

Yet it's funny how even the simplest dreams
all too often go unrealized.

Cadence Beckons the Willow

Breeze curls at the lip of the weeping willow
      Tendrils green as chocolate lime candies
Cascading down to earth in
             apology

For its faithful sway, dappled in sun
Inflections pure as the Queen's English

I capture the view from my bedroom window
and *reminisce* the blessings of a thousand summer days
Beneath its cool shade, as cadence
           beckoned the willow

Mink Coat

It was the signature style
of a woman who held value.
Someone special,
he always wanted you to know
that you were his everything.

A mink coat was not for every day,
just special moments
snatched in celebration.
Dinner for two,
romance and candlelight.

Capturing everything in its folds,
    the essence of you
could be traced in its silk lining.
Passed between my palms,
softness tempting me to touch, too much.

Your familiar scent of
jasmine with a hint of bergamot
could be pulled back from yesterday
every time, I buried my face
in the indulgence of fur and memories.

Dizzy in Ribbons

ribbons, so many
    too many to count
      I could weave
        blankets of them
        stitch a new world
        between picot edges
      an ocean of colours
      that could drown
    me in a sea, then
  craft a safety net
from the herringbone
lines easing me
  across turning tides
    ribbons, so many
      like guide ropes
        as I navigate and
        tread new waters
        just over the horizon
      dizzied by ribbons
    a velvet tease with
feathered edging
jewel colours twinkle
  distract my wondering
    eyes that never cast
      upon the fading light
      my vanishing point
    past which the water
undoubtedly must fall

A Night Out—In Your Shoes

Will I warm my curls with the dryer
nails coated in cinnabar
legs smooth with a hint of black
atop, pinched with clips and ribbon
shocking in stockings like you?

Will I bristle powder pink and blue
across my eyes too, then
puff my cheeks with rouge tones
a spritz of florals at my nape
to accentuate your English rose?

Will I slip my feet into open toe
stiletto heels that clip clop
black and gold straps that criss cross
until fastened at my ankle
making me taller than waist high?

Will I have a true love hold me
close and smile that smile
he saves only for you, and yours for him
to take me dining and dancing
and make me feel like grown-ups do?

Will I walk on the arm of the proudest man
be the prize for his eyes
and laugh in love like the two of you do?
Sometimes I just can't wait
to be a woman and walk in your shoes.

We Spoke in Crush Tones

We spoke of a young girl's crush,
a rite of passage.
Wrapped in the easy chair they call
mother and *daughter*.

We imagined pastel-tinted moments,
talked through the rules of play,
lost ourselves within
the transition of times changing.

And we dreamed my future,
just ahead it lay in wait.
Worlds built on a day
you would never get to see.

To the Beat of the Eton Rifles

The water tank always ran cold on Friday nights.
Sometimes it was better, especially
for shrinking drainpipe denim.
Weekend track changes marked
by Kinks and The Jam,
and a place you said was Motown.
As mysterious to me as your Winklepicker boots
and your button down shirt.
A revivalist of the sub-culture.
The working class dandies for want of a better label,
and it was all about the labels then.

Your parka sidestepped military life in favour of
the Eton Rifles, their beat reverberating
as it followed you out of the door, oh brother.
Moving from lad to man, quick as you can.
I'd note your style, boyish frame in sharp suit,
long and tall, freckles framing your charm.
Then wait in shadow for your return, listen in
laugh along. Try to play pool as you tried
to shake me off, cramping your style, always.
Rivalry at times, but rarely unraveled, even so.
A fire in your eyes, just like hers, that lit up
when you walked in the room,
an idol of sorts, or so it seemed to me.

VOLUME 2

SALTED NOTES &
TRANSITION VERSES

Whispers

Round and round
In whispers they go
Think I don't know
My ear to the ground

Hear crackles, electric
In whispers they go
Think I don't know
Though it makes me sick

(with worry) the half truths
In whispers I found
Unsure of each sound
Something. But no proof

The foreboding intense
In whispers I found
Unsure of each sound
Feelings make no sense

Love Locked In

You came to me
in the earliest days of January

Unfurled palm revealing
precious treasure

A lock of your hair

Snippet of conker
bound in raspberry satin

To remember me

I didn't know
why
I should

Silver reflected in your eyes
as you took a swirl
of mine in black

To take with me

I didn't know
where
you were going

A Song for Two

Their song spoke
of true love ways
in a cradle caught
between this rock
and a harder place

As piano keys tripped
over teardrops
held in the dark

Time carried them
along the twists and turns
the rollercoaster

She, his forever lady
(in hand-stitched cotton)
He, the sentry come forth
(in cowboy boots)

To topple the unthinkable
until, more bearable now
salt water turned to wine

Under powdered moon
shine (they two)

Tender scars
wrapped in mink kisses

And turning in, to
skintight embrace
face to face
heart to heart
Why worry now?

Maybe there would be blue sky
after this grey

Though the worm
still burrows

And so this love song
must come to an end

Calendar Days

It must have been late September.
When you first heard the words
that ring fenced your future.

The root of a ravenous weed
growing in your breast, making
home of your womanhood.

Through the white corridors of October
I spied squares of yellowed skin,
became disaffected by disinfectant smells.

November muttered conversations
that eliminated a thing called mas-tec-to-my.
I couldn't help but wonder what it all meant.

The bitterness of December
must have deposited the rot, gift wrapped
in a bag full of Christmas shopping.

Finally you doubled over, in the shoe store
as I recall it. I observed. Unclear why the adults
tilted their heads and blue lights rushed in.

By late January you cried out in the night and I
would move to rescue, then retreat to shadow
as the beast was hidden by a morphine blanket.

At the calendar's turn you emerged in rare lucidity
to ask *Am I going to die?* I had answers now, but was
ushered out as curtains pulled around your bed.

I've no idea how he told you, perhaps
he didn't need to, our crumpled faces spoke the words
of a conversation ended with the cold kiss of February.

Ending . . . Then Begins Again

A phone call drifts through the wall.
The clockworks stall at five a.m.
Don't need to hear the words
I know. Wait for the door to open
but harsh light bounces in.

This is the end, so let's begin.

Off we go, scooped from sleep,
too tired to weep, yet . . .
Funny how the songs that
crackle through the radio
seem to know your truth
before you realise it hurts.

I pluck the lyrics, easily
like picking ripe cherries
from a baseless bowl.
Hard stones choking back
the words, unshared
because none make sense.

Silently we trip, sharing
in our isolation, trapped.

Let's go back.

Pretend.
Delay the end, full stop.

Get off this rollercoaster
leading us out of control.

No recompense for this
Mother's last kiss
at this moment, so with
legs buckling, I move
as the floor falls away.

Can't do this today.

Keep British upper lips stiff.
Don't let grief rip
at your sides, pour out
the acrid tears of the ferocious
beast the adults call grief.
So I am still, wondering how.

I see her, but she's not there.
Like a life, but the brightness
turned down. Drowned out
by morphine drip.

With trembled lip, I say
Goodbye

with no idea
just what would release
the flow, the force
that was rushing at the back.
I feel numb, undone.
How could I know?
At the end. Of the beginning.

What yet to meet me?

But wait;
you'll see how this pans out.

All that remains now,
a messy wound drifting
towards decay, turning
gangrenous with loss.

The abandoned battlefield
strewn with dismembered
lives.

Full stops amid
the rot of grieving hearts.

A Conversation of Unspeakable Loss

watching you, prone, chalk
so many questions fluttering
mysteries unspoken, unheard
and so I breathe melodies
across your closed eyes
with every note, I pause
await the echoes of you
words spilt just for me
but silence takes my breath

I feel you close
taste the salt of your tears
blend them with sweet honey drops
released from the rainbows
I swaddle you with, as I
walk you through the colours
the ones you sang to me
that afternoon in pigtails
I heard you then, hear you still

fear forms like moth balls
finding first home in me
strange, new, and unclear
creasing my soft brow
as I tilt my head
searching at the bedside
for traces, clues, what now?
only a mother's lullaby to comfort

rock-a-bye child
hush-a-bye, for no worries
smooth sorrows trail
chase it with a caress
of the sun on moist cheeks
rock-a-bye child
hush-a-bye, for no worries
the yellow brick road
waits for you still
follow it brick by brick

I will walk in the shadows and reach for you

I will be a lantern at your side as you search

Running With the Ball

Next morning as I strolled
in the wake of your memories

Placid waters moved to tremble

Reflections emerged
through the sediment ripples

Peering in a new dawning gifted me
with panic, to roll between heavy hands

Unseen, but a choice made too clear

Dutifully I submitted my weakness
as nourishment to a fear-formed ball

My tender mouth readily swallowing
as it scratched; dry toast to raw throat

Before taking root in my solar plexus

And I knew we were in it together
No running, just travelling long haul

Thoughts of Last Summer

We'd walked together one afternoon
no explanation for our visit
to the cemetery overlooking the park
just the gentle warm breeze
winding us through the imposing oaks
that bordered the church and its grounds

You were elegant, soft with respectful calm
me, carefree and skip-along, just another girl
the hazy sunlight offering a glow that I'd imagined
was God himself stretching out long fingers
to stroke the headstones; comfort the grieving

Small grey paving stones led us in squares
past the wartime memorials
carpeted with poppies so red
it looked as though the ground was bleeding
gentle sorrow breaking the monotone

We turned right and then left
past the unkempt concrete tombs
perished after decades without care
turned left again and we were wandering
amongst the high mounds of disturbed earth
fresh wreaths and flowers abound

Row upon row of devoted wives and mothers
darling husbands and fathers, sons and daughters
a parade of angels sitting on gilded pedestals
asleep, or *at peace, with God,* or *sadly passed*
not one dared to offer explanation for the last breath

Neither of us had a reason for being there
our next steps still to be trodden
it was just where our fate had lead us that day
so we followed with trusting hearts
unaware that we would meet here again
but that was last summer, now I stand in solitude.

Lost on the Front Pew

I can't recall the weather
so I'll presume that it was drenched
with monochromes of pewter
air perfumed with morbid stench

I can't recall what I was wearing
except a heavy shawl of loss
tied with a sash of my unbearing
edged with single rose to toss

I can't recall the quivered sighs
of mourners singing low
in muttered chorus of goodbyes
somber tears as verses flow

I can't recall the faces
that surrounded me that day
just the grief-folded embraces
of mourners chasing blues away

I can't recall the precious view
of remnant family seated by
just feeling lost on the front pew
her final resting fixed my eye

I can't recall such feelings
nor make sense of being slave
to woe and all its dealings
standing wretched by the grave

Jewel Drops

Diamonds drip
From feathered lashes
Their raw edges grip
My eyes
A mist descends
But blinking back
The sadness, pretends

I swallow, I'm weak
The diamonds
Roll down, stain cheek
Resting
At the corner of my lip
To nothing but a scratch
In my throat as I sip

All Change Please

family and friends I'd loved for a lifetime
stepped out as fresh starts
laid their bait in shark infested waters
circling the irreparable holes in my safety net

A Do Over

If I were you, what would I have done?
There was a time I used to think
that I would have sliced off my arms and legs,
set fire to my hair, just to be there.

Unable to understand why you didn't
fight more, fall harder, get back up.

If I were you, what would I have done?
There was a time I used to think
that not telling the children
was preserving secrets in cellophane.

Nobody else had the right to know,
I was damn sure I had the right.

If I were you, what would I have done?
There was a time I used to think
that I would have captured every moment
in a freeze frame of soft focus sepia.

Before stowing it in a memory box
deep in the dust pile under the bed.

If I were you, what would I have done?
There was a time I used to think
that you got it wrong for me at least,
now I am not so sure. I realise you protected me

and as decay took you over, so it was that I could
set you pretty on my mantelpiece of lost treasures

Given Half a Chance

Given half a chance
I would have filled the void
smiled and hummed the day away
cleaning up the mess
filling up the kitchen
with smells of Sunday roast
or home burnt toast
and that would have been good enough
because cooking wasn't her forte

Given half a chance
I could have been like her
made you happy over breakfast
topped up your flask with tea
sent you off to work
been there to greet you at the end
smothered you in squeezed hugs
and fresh white laundry
that you'd turn pink with your efforts

Given half a chance
I should have been afforded
the opportunity to try
to be the lady of the house
care for us with her motherly love
be the sticking plaster
to our common wound
the nourishment we needed
but it simply wouldn't do

Given half a chance
she wouldn't
have got
her
foot
in
the
door

Saving Your Seat

in February you stepped out
and I saved your seat at the table,
by June another woman's feet
were tapping the tiles underneath it

Hello Stranger

Curious on first meet
You look like a mother
But not mine

Pale skin, brunette yes
You look like a mother
But not mine

Circling you I see it now
You look like a mother
But not mine

Straighter lines, different shape
You look like a mother
But not mine

Child at your side, younger
You look like her mother
But not mine

A friend, a caregiver maybe
You look like a mother
But not mine

Smaller eye, thinner lip
You look like a mother
But not mine

Disobedient stride gives you away
You are a mother, yes
But nothing like mine

You stand at his side, too close
You are not my mother
You'll never be mine

Another World

At first she would visit after school,
swept in on a cloud of bleach and
scouring pad smiles, shifting the dust
before sorting the laundry and later on
conjuring the breath of home cooked meals.

She quickly learned what you liked and
served it up on a gilt edged platter.
Cleaner now free of a bad marriage
of bruises and forked tongue twists.
Come to polish our veneer.

Heavy footed and hardworking, stepped
off the bus from the council estate
and into our house. Never asking a penny
more than her wage and yet, she took.
Everything we had, sucked into the vacuum.

In her hand she held a ransom note
for a safe return I could never afford alone.
Her world resided somewhere in the cheap seats,
built unstable on the aisles of the discount stores.
Pile it high; sell it low but everything has a cost.

She took us along for the ride and
all the while I blinked back and choked hard
unable to figure out how we'd got here,
where she had come from and how she'd
blown open the worm holes that disconnected us.

My world had been a garden of lavender and herbs,
soft hands in warm folds and spun sugar smiles,
gingham topped jars and feather down blankets.
But she walked in so fast and so purposefully,
I had no time to salvage my supplies and run for cover.

Aliens Have Landed

Aliens have landed.
They walk among us,
but strangers
          (to me).
Unseeing eyes
looking back at mine.

Not versed in our ways,
who says what, and when.
So. Begin again?

New language to learn.
Who follows? Who leads?
What to believe, except this.
Accept this?
As you plant a kiss,
your hand on his knee,
but you, so alien to me.

Planetary shifts as
new life drifts over craters.
Wallpapers over cracks,
no going back.

Dawn of a new earth.
All change.
Rules of a game not yet played.

I'll take my bat and ball,
stall for a while,
slow progress, digress,
create diversion that
submerges my distress.

Moon rocks
in response
to the pull of gravity
that does not hold me.

As I stabilise,
(try to) acclimatise,
to this new occupancy
of alien territory.
It's just not me!
Not mine!

So I decline.

Rebel.

Show all is

not well.

Now aliens have landed.

Road Kill #1

On a hot day in June
you invited her to come
burst my bubble gum ideals

Too afraid to speak your own truth
you thought it was a cargo
best docked by a woman

You don't mind that we
are seeing each other do you?

And the stench of pineapple chunks
on sticks, pricked at my bile
as I watched your lips move

There it was, the silent hunter
stowed in the back of a high speed truck
that hit me without warning

VOLUME 3
BITTER BALLADS & HARD BEATS

Cleanse me

Every time I watch you put your hand on his knee
the blue bottles swarm around the abscess you suture
and I want to purge myself of everything you are to me

Everything You Are

Everything you are
is everything she wasn't.
She had apples at her cheeks
whilst yours are razor sharp.
The hourglass she oozed
is lost in your straight lines.
An artist's easel was silk 'tween her fingers
whilst Brillo roughs your knuckles.
I'll always wonder if that's why
he chose you; for your differences.
In the end she was irreplaceable.

Psychic Babble

She believed in the other side
and I was curious to know, whilst he
was a skeptic in search of salvation.

The words of her friend, her medium,
always spelt the truth she foretold
(or what she made it if she tried hard enough),
and I was curious to know.

My narcissist emerging then,
What of me, what of me? What would I be?
Que sera sera you used to sing in my ear.
So tell me, through psychic babble
what will I be? But the future's not ours to see
(Didn't you say that too?).

But she promised revelations
from the lips of a charlatan.
No doubt to self-assure
that turning down the volume
on voices of the past was fine,
and I was curious to know.

We were all searching (or was it just me?)
to find the truths in our lies,
push past the smoke and mirrors.
More agendas than a board room.

And I was curious to know
as I sneaked a peek through
scribbled notes of affirmation
allegedly written by you,
channeled by her pen (is that true?).
Was everything really going to be okay?

I Always Wanted a Sister

Has anyone ever told you to be careful what you wish for?
There's a lesson in here somewhere, I'm sure of that much.
I always wanted a sister, I just didn't imagine
that it would come about this way, forced
family ties with loose knots that could only come undone.

There you were one day, sitting in the living room,
legs crossed in white socks, face pale and silent,
six years old with an eye patch, glasses, braided hair,
and somewhat unexpectedly my revulsion for our situation
abated as this dream came true, lost girls me and you.

It wasn't your fault or mine, we were the wallpaper
pasted to the white noise, fighting to be heard
through muted speakers in a family show home.
I looked out for you, I looked forward to you
and when you stayed over I could understand.

I knew why you hated it when they kissed or held hands.
Truth be told it made us both squirm but we couldn't say,
our protestations unwelcome at this table, so in the end
you played your hand of wild cards. And despite the fact
that we were not related, they looked a lot like mine.

Life in the Snow Globe

At times it was like sitting in a snow globe.
A hand bigger than any of ours
twisting and turning, everything jumbled
before shaking it up to watch us drown,
as the storm spat plumes of white all around.
So much going on within its madness, and
chaos at a glance as sky flurries by.
But at the center, figures stood as still life
in pose they were created for, but no souls.
Just vacant stares and hand-painted smiles,
our lights extinguished by tiny tornado swirls
encased within the sphere of glass.
No sound penetrates. Just silent lips,
our mouths the only things left dry.

Road Kill #2

At twelve years old I sneaked downstairs
eased open the lounge door and
saw the two of you entwined on the carpet.
Legs embroiled in the new possibilities
and the headlights shone at my bare feet.

At thirteen years old I sat amid a throng of grown women
as they passed around frilled viscose and nylon
in provocative tones as putrid as stale marriages,
and a woman I didn't know told me to stop
giving you a hard time. I didn't hear the air horn
warning of the engine roar at my back.

At fourteen years old I picked through the closets, knowing
it was none of my business, but snooping becomes
so seductive when you've lingered in the dark for too long.
Perhaps I shouldn't have been hurt when I found
the temptress's trail of love and lust and unsightly stuff
where my mother's mink coat used to hang. But the truck
knocked me flat, the wheels leaving imprints as they rolled over me.

Winter's Advance

And there I was unfastened, suspended
Caught mute amongst the madness
As winter snatched my cape of fleece, pulled at my bobble hat
Until I stood exposed, dressed only in English lace and shivers

Arresting Development

Four girls window shopping
That's all it was meant to be
Excited at the prospect
of stretching out the seams
mixing tie-dyes with tiaras
as hard house beats
poured on to the shop floor

But in all the commotion
things got muddled
Bags left unchecked and
suspicions aroused, erratic behaviour
Security alerted and soon
we were detained, then dispensed
out on the street, police in tow

The irony of all of this
was that you came to my rescue
Though there wasn't any need
Not this time; not this day
But you defended my name,
called out in complaint
until honour was restored

No child of mine will be branded a thief
Indignant at the suggestion
that I could bring such disrepute
You didn't know, didn't want to see
that there was another day
and many more after that (guilty I plead)
I called for you but you never came again

A Place of Men and Boys

As a small child I had felt the acceptance of female love and compassion, covered in icing sugar and kisses by a collective of aunties, neighbours, and friends. Protected at the center; a butterfly in a crystal cocoon. Now I found myself at odds in a place where only men and boys would walk, speaking with harsh tones or muffled sighs I couldn't understand. Every time I opened my mouth to speak they seemed unaware that my lips were moving, or unable to hear my rounded sounds. The rhythm of high heels now served only as an alarm warning of the coming of a woman forced to be mine.

The women I had known, held close, who held me closer, seemed to be slipping through my fingers. The friends I'd had were fading faster having lost interest in my needy status as the motherless gooseberry. In time many of my girlfriends twisted their faces, whilst the others turned away not knowing how to handle me or what to say.

I needed to find somewhere I could be tolerated, understood, heard, and accepted, and so I started looking . . . in all the wrong places.

Battle Cries

You said you'd scar my face
>   *(and I was afraid)*

With rings, to crush my heart and other things
>   *(just wanted to run)*

You never said why we went from friends
>   *(will someone make it stop)*

To wish I was dead, no time for amends
>   *(wish they could change this)*

Your eyes black with soot, heavy boot on foot
>   *(screaming for help, from inside out)*

Come to trample on my shine
>   *(if only I could hide)*

Force me back to shadow
>   *(under blanket, not coming out)*

Take the pride I might define
>   *(don't want to go to school tomorrow)*

You took the air from my lungs
>   *(no breathing space left)*

Cut the words from my tongue

       (you couldn't hear my tears)

Lead an army in your battle against my existence

       (I fought alone, unarmed)

Until all the doors were closed in

       (nowhere else for me to go)

The Quizzical Matter of Women & Girls

Once you were gone, very little made sense
about girls like me and women like you.
Maybe that was it, they weren't like you and I.
Or I was not like them and you? I can't be sure.

I don't think I follow, but I know this much
I've figured. There are no good girls and bad girls,
just girls with unending capacity to harm
themselves and each other.
A glint in the eyes of beware or be gone.

You look like me, we share common ground
as we stand side by side in virgin skin and
freshly washed hair resting on our shoulders.
We laugh, sing, dance in front of the mirror,
impress each other, practice and preen for the lovers
we would grow to attract one day.

Until the element of competition strolls in
between, causing cracks in the pavement we laid
together once upon a time.
Is it our mothers' legacy that we now play hand in hand
with steely daggers behind our backs?

A girly girl right through to my dresses and your heels.
And yet so little made sense to me in all this.
I didn't fit right in like I should have.
Popularity trumps the misshapen soul every time.
So if not one of them, who am I to be?
My identity held in code, mine to decipher
someday, perhaps in days of womanhood I'd find.

My lens shows the women in a different light
since revealed as the takers or the taken.
Mother turned in to the mother earth, as
father and brother turned into women's arms.
Whilst I hold my own, hands outstretched,
for not even God knows who or what I seek.
Where to begin when your frame of reference
is long gone?

Denial

Did you choose?
(I hope you didn't)

Was it you who denied
the doctors as they tried
to suggest a course?

I thought I heard you say
that to lose your hair
would be too much
that the slicing of a breast
would be detestable
but less than death

Did you choose?
(I hope you didn't)

Was it you who denied
the doctors as they tried
to suggest a course?

You spoke to your friend
I was there and I know
she said it could be done
then reconstructed with ease
and you said you would
do exactly as you pleased

Did you choose?
(I hope you didn't)

Was it you that denied
the doctors as they tried
to suggest a course?

Fragments of your voice
haunt my memories as they
suggest that maybe you chose
vanity over life, but that can't be
and who am I to judge the value
placed on dying with dignity

Did you choose?
(I hope you didn't)

Was it you that denied
the doctors as they tried
to suggest a course?

I would cut off all my limbs
to lie next to you again
take the last locks of my hair
they'd be needless without you
there
perhaps it was too late for you
to try dismemberment and poison

But I *would* choose
(*I'd* choose *you*)

So, was it you that denied
or is it me trying to hide
my rage in empty reasons?

Soundtrack of Silence

The music died with you, leaving only the crackle of vinyl.
Broken melodies played out in fever high pitch, calling you home
for an encore that was disturbed as earth pulled you underground.

Our bridge over troubled waters collapsed and we remained
only in the echoes, like a gentle hum reverberating through the amp.
The beat ceased as the band rolled out of town, and I waited in the rain.

Until the day they took your pictures away, stowed your memorabilia
and I sat in a new stillness with litter at my feet as the lights went down.
Time to go home, but you were home (to me) and I had no place else
to go.

After that I never picked over the piano keys, couldn't find my voice
in the sheet music now stalled, pages unturned by my hand and I wish
I could go back and find our tune, then learn to play it to the end.

Pulling the Veil

I was becoming a pain in the ass,
of that I have no doubt.
Pulling pig tails, pulling punches,
and pulling veils over your eyes
every time you said no.

I was going to do it anyway
to see how close I could get to the edge
before you would come and take my hand.
So I can see why you sat, numb.
Deflated and paralytic with apathy.

It was too much. I was too much.
You'd all said it, and I'd heard you often.
I couldn't have agreed more,
the lid on the pressure cooker
trembling with rage before explosion.

Sometimes you'd get close enough
to see the shadows through the voile.
Much as I wanted you to walk right in,
I didn't know how to offer the invitation,
so instead I'd feel for another distortion.

Dance the dance, stretch and spin,
weave my web until you gave up again.
You were strong, but my will was stronger.
Ask your Dad she'd say; and even as a young child
you were the soft touch and I'd get my way if I pushed.

So why stop now? Because I wanted to,
but I could not give in despite the futility of the fight.
I'd lace up my gloves, jump in for another round
and leave you hanging on the ropes.
Always looking back to see if you'd fight for me.

The Water Fight

It had only been about a year since you'd passed
The smiles were slowly creeping back across our faces,
there were even days when things seemed normal
For a second there I was fooled into thinking
that everything might just turn out all right

Once again a call came through
as we frolicked in the garden, a water fight
to cool the intense heat of a dry summer
Grandma Dot was gone, life evaporated with the water,
her heart eventually broken as we both wished mom was here

Good Girl

My lungs fill with the ash of grief.
I don't want to be a good girl.
I want to smash my nice manners.
Take my turn. Tell my tale.
Force you to watch the scene unfold.
And I hope it hurts. I hope you feel.
I hope you notice.

Walking in the Rain

I was awe struck, star struck even
as I walked into the wake of your rebellion
You were older than me, just a little
Sauntered with a swagger in your step
Street smart with a razor's edge
I knew you'd be the one
Brazenly, I encouraged and invited
your attentions, always welcome

Tinfoil raindrops glittered against street lamps
Restless with stage fright at first
Cold brick scratching sharp at my back
then warmed by a single shot from hip
you pulled me into your night
For the first time, I closed my eyes
and dropped my white ribbons to the floor

empty

thoughts won't form more
than scattered white pepper in my head
mouth can't round the sounds
where words used to be
nothing is clear anymore
unsure of what is here anymore
am I empty, unlovable?
or do you not love me like you should?

Oh Brother Where Art Thou?

Waiting in your shadow, I hope of your return.
These days you come back less and less.
When you do there are only shards of you.
The pointed edges of the puzzle we all were.
The curves and cul-de-sacs that fit together
once upon a time, back when. Back then.
Now we spit bitter pennies,
the currency of our dispute.
Traded on serrated tongues,
bartering over our disillusionment
at what was lost, forever.
Yet what is lost? So much more
than you or I could express to each other
or the shells of ourselves, that lie,
washed up on the shifting sands
of our bleakest springtime together.

Fell the Mighty Oak

It takes a surgeon to fell a tree
like me, but at times you
were the master of the art.
New buds emerged
from my outstretched fingers.
Sap coursing through
to quench my thirst for more.
And all too often
you would seek to cut.
Curtail the growth,
the flex and bend
that moved me into sun
(or dappled shade at the least).
Dreams are made like that,
take root in a hundred years.
History turned to bright future,
yet to dim my light was just enough
to deter my passions
and poison the gifts I gave.

Angry Ambassador

You'd charge at me without questions
Just accusations and indifferent attitude
Something to despise, like gum on the sole of a boot
Difficult to get rid of, a constant reminder
of a time when it all went wrong

As I remember it, my presence seemed to stir conflict
Emotions driven by your strong head and a family script
A tale of loyalty written in indelible ink
My protector with an inherent need for rejection
Siblings who couldn't share loss over such distance

The sadness lies in everything you thought I was
The irony lies in the notion that I wasn't drowning when
you waded into unchartered waters, fighting to keep me afloat
It was only when you eventually turned your back
that I sank to the bottom and drowned anyway

The Salon

I wanted the look, her look of back comb
and polished black, the one I had seen shining
from the black and white photograph
preserved behind sticky back cellophane

Taken back in the day when it was
just those two, and not even my brother
was reflected from the shine in their eyes
Already an image of her, I wanted to sharpen the focus

So I sat in the chair and I asked for what she was
When I stepped through the front door I wanted him
to remember what was missing, even if the
remembering hurt so much his heart might burst again

Daisy Chains

Plucking daisies, here, there
Everywhere
Clear liquid seeps
As I dig my nails in
Piercing the stalks
Shocks of green lines intertwine

Linking chains, here, there,
Everywhere
Slipping through the cracks
White and yellow bursts
Lying on my belly, no cares
But last summer's daisy chains

Attaching strands, here, there
Everywhere
Wrapped around fingers
Dangling from soft tendrils
Of midnight black hair
Tickling tender skin, last summer

And now I lie, here, there
Everywhere
Lines stretched out front
But yellows and greens recede
Only powder white lines, I spy
Through child's eyes, watching

Searching in the rushes, here, there
Everywhere
Surges trickle through my veins
Pulling me under the waves
I languish, conflicted, stranded
Between here and last summer

Nobody holding on, here, there
Everywhere
So I let go, fall back
On chemical comforts, left wanting
Until crashing, I hit the bottom
The daisies turned to dust

Dancing Daze

My dancing days came rushing in
with amphetamine urgency
A lost face in an overwhelming crowd
Rave rhythms pulsating through my ribs
like my heart would burst right out
Maybe it would have, but I had self-control
knew the limits of sniffing and popping
Kept on dancing, kept on smiling
as euphoria took me crowd surfing
before falling back into the mosh pit
Things could get hot and heavy there
It was then I would close my eyes
try to feel for one more rush

Have you ever tried dancing with your eyes closed?

Colours pass through the lens
shapes move in then recede
as you walk upside down in the sky
You are relentless, no boundaries
when the music stops, there's nothing left
just skin like warm milk and being fourteen
Back in your school uniform by Monday
pencil tapping to the beat of another weekend

Sinking Into Silhouettes

Dark slashes the twilight
   Splits the night's approach
Dividing the have, and the
    had   too   much. The last taste
as Thunderbirds fortifies the grip
   of my spiral laid down and out
stretched flat, like empty canvas
   Dirt and leaves at my back
Flames licking as I sink in
   to the bottle, in hot pursuit
Friends fade out to silhouette
   Echoes of past and present meld yet
nothing penetrates this numb heart
   Even as it rains black arrows
and the sky falls in again with every drop

Sun Kissed the Peaches

The foreign sun stretched its fingers
and bent to kiss my open skin
the first night I wandered the bars
in women's shoes
Body hugging jersey,
black with neon powder prints
stretched over new hips and thighs
made shapes like honey drizzles
My toasted shoulders ablaze
bare and there for the taking
as the white spots that hid
under peach satin and frills
the thrill of dark eyes
and darker strangers still
to stir curiosity in me
And as cut glass
laced with Ouzo traced my lips
with anise, I displayed
more than my fifteen years
Or at least he thought, and so
I played the game, snookered
until closing time, last orders
What can I get you? I'll take you home
So I went willingly but
once shrouded in the cloak
of a cheap fling, my confidence left
as my inexperience emerged
Tear stains stripe my tender face
at this contemptible cocktail

A bitter taste on my tongue
my heart too young, began to race
as I searched in the shadows
for a way out of the night
Safer instead to lie in wait
and then, as dawn crept in
and my lover snoozed his conquest
away in dreams of smug satisfaction
I felt for the door in whispers
When you wake up, I'll be gone
The breaking heat and crickets
walked hand in hand with my shame
In bare feet and last night's scent
I wondered how I came to be
alone with the Grecian sunrise
Somebody take me home

Bring Me to Life

slumped face down in linoleum moments
I struggle to find the life inside
to lift from this spot
so maybe I'll just stay here
and let my intensity
leave scorch marks
on the floor of this crime scene

Where Have All the Adults Gone?

Reaching for safe arms.
My keepers embrace, I climb in
longing for response
from faces once smiling.
Beguiling me with kind eyes
once, but soon gone.
There was a father, but now nowhere
to be found, I watch and wait,
create fuss and frolic
in the hope of notice
that again your kind eyes
would rest on mine.

See inside the pain
that remains (it always will).
In dark tunnels, no light breaks,
thieves just take, innocence lost.
Circling opportunities to fill
the void, the fossil of my soul.
Not part of a whole, alone and
so I stir, more than before,
running in rings, seeing things,
your child knowing, growing.

Too much, too young, strung
out on powders and potions,
emotions ride the toxic wave,
illogical ideals, but you won't see,
can't see, don't want to, where are you?

We are all victims
of our circumstances, in trances
we move through the days,
weeks, and years recede,
our bond dissipates,
lies in wait of return, and I yearn
in optimistic hope that I get
to feel you turn cheek to mine.

Hear my unsaid truth, share
the damages and ravages
of our toppled pedestal, falling
crumpled and unsure, roses
around the door, now closed.

Me on one side, you on the other,
aching to reach, have you teach me again,
calling for you, eternity uttered.
Yet eyes and ears are sealed,
layers of salty sadness wash over,
 in drowning we share so much,
 but still can't touch.

The words not on tips of tongues,
nor front of mind. So you be kind
to yourself forsaking the rest.
But this test of will and strength
was unknown before our sky fell.
What's right and wrong, anybody
and nobody can guess, suggest
the right path to follow forward
that will lead us to lighter, brighter.

Days, turning to dark nights,
frightened at times, alone writing
letters, I can't find the sounds.

Words just hit the ground running,
scared of reply, of resigned sighs.
So we avoid, are redeployed.
New lives, lovers, beginnings
from endings.

Except for me
still waiting,
wondering.
Where have all the adults gone?

Behind the Headlines

I want you to look at me
from behind newspaper headlines,
TV guide, and a five day forecast

If I reached for you I fear that
the fire running through my restless fingers
would ignite the crumpled tinder pages
leaving you with nothing but embers
and ashes, so I sit on the other side of the room
in the hope I'll catch your eye one day

The Bubble Man

Here comes the bubble man, blowing
A glimpse in between sleight of hand
Pushing promises, leading me, at first
    By fist,
        then hand,
            then finger tips link

And slowly . . . I follow, one foot
then another
Unseeing, unknowing
but ever so
Think I know where I tread,
although

Step changes carry me away
The dance starts up in spin, turning
at a pace as I dive, fate first into him
Deceitful in his craft, sprinkles glitter
in my wide eyes, the almonds he finds sweet
He sweeps with long limbs, topples me
then keeps me afloat with melodies and
madness   finds me wanting,
willingly
. . . I
. . . go

Step forward once more, then before I lie
I whisper lost words in the air
to be found here, but I'm not there
if they come looking. Gone, as I dared
Who cares?
Not anymore, I'm dancing
with the bubble man, he rushes on

Face pops in mine, and I am epiphyte
taking root, unable to free myself
So I keep up with the follow
Blind at the dawn of my emergence
into womanhood with him and yet still

A girl's heart beats within, trapped
unable to find safe passage out or route back
Development   dis-rup-ted, mistrust placed
with a hunger, a greed for the heaviest anchor

And so I followed you, under the archways
A child,
in,
thigh high. Why?

Through doorways into worlds, windows obscured
so they can't see, how they'd disagree

Vulnerability unearthed and peeled back as
you and me, veer off track. Together?
Or just one? Enthralled by the pied piper

Will I ever get back?
Who would catch me?
Clothe me again, in short socks and ribbons
not woman's cloak. I'm not.
Can't you see?
Nor me.
How could I?
Carried
    off
        in
            a
                bubble

A Question of Who's to Blame

I don't want to have to explain it to you, but
you want to know why I was so willing,
complicit in my shame.
Don't you?

You want to know why I walked into an underworld
at tender age, hands linked with his easily,
teased into illicit endeavours.
Don't you?

You want to know
why I wrapped myself sticky and sweet in shiny black
and stretched lace, zipped to barely there.
Don't you?

You want to know if I got found out
as I pulled layers of chenille over my head,
rolled high at my neck to cover the signs of slut.
Don't you?

My delicate skin put on the show
of an old pro, and you want to know why
I lay in his small room of big expectations.
Don't you?

You want to know why, under lava light,
I let him come find me as I stared in wonder,
stolen as my seedy shadow reflected on the wall
Don't you?

He was older than me, of course,
and you want to know why
the petulant child in me said yes instead of no.
Don't you?

You want to know why I hitched up my school skirt,
let him climb inside, in the back of his car,
only the steam on the windows to shield me.
Don't you?

You surely want to know why, if I was a smart girl,
did I drop my teddy bears and PJs
as quickly as my morals.
Don't you?

You want to know
where were the parents? Didn't they see?
Why did nobody intervene?
Don't you?

And I'll have to disappoint you,
because I simply don't have the answers.

Looking the Other Way

I fell into you,
not *in love* with you.
My wanton eyes
unable to see
who entered stage left
as I tumbled
underwater, swimming.
Didn't want to come up for air.
Searching in the scrub,
for the love of comfort.
Cold flannel to my fever,
but nothing to be found.
So deeper I went,
sunk, drunk on you,
and love, your lies.
Smokescreen smiles
that curled until
cherry bitten,
smitten and so,
I fell into you
not *in love* with you.
Must have happened when
I was looking the other way.

Through the Doors

In the music of that night you asked
C'mon baby light my fire
You gotta love your man (so I did)
In the only way I knew, you'd taught
Strutted my stuff, no name for it
Not from my lips anyway
Just a girl, in your favorite, red
nails and lace, the roses you gave
Petals peeled from gentle buds
The music played a siren's call
And the nights went on forever
Looking back through wiser eyes
I wish I'd never opened to The Doors
just gone home for tea instead

Night Terrors

They dropped me off outside your house
I knocked, and waited in the dark
We'd planned it to the letter
but you must have failed to cross a *t*
or dot the *i*, because the house was in black
by the time I arrived at three a.m.

My cover was a girly sleepover
They bought my story, and again I don't know why
suspicions grew harder to arouse these days

I didn't panic at first, just banged a little louder
You were expecting me so I was sure you'd answer
then I sat a while on the door step
The night getting darker in this rough part of town
where you rented a house with the guys and
the cold grew colder, so I hammered this time

A little girl somewhere inside me got scared
whilst the rebel refused to give up easy and so
walking a mile in unfamiliar heels I found a payphone

You didn't hear the telephone, you didn't hear the door
Maybe you heard me crying like a baby
emptying my self-respect into the gutter as the rain started
Clinging on to the belief that you loved me
Giving you the benefit of the doubt
Praying you weren't whispering secrets behind closed doors (I'm afraid
of those)

Once I got inside, you were apologetic and I didn't ask questions
You'd fallen asleep and I was just grateful
that you didn't have another girl in bed with you

Now I know I should have been asking so much more for myself

Finding Your Face in Mine

Searching for me in you, you in me
Curve of brow, but not mine I see

For who is she?

Someone I know not, forgot
Shooting arrows from bow

Of berried lip

Tracing lines with velvet tip
Moon shaped, with high cheek

Bones, no home

Piercing eyes not recognised
As mine, yet once upon a time

I was there

In the mirror as I stare, looking
Bounced back a reflective trace

Can't name the face

Now found haunting the hollows
Fleeting, in moments I emerge

Ghosted, moving

In directions not signposted
I seek, to find your face in mine

Mine in yours

Where My Loyalties Lie

There's a fondness for you
Something I can't deny
I was raised to respect my elders
So I had to find a way
In spite of myself

After all these years
I still can't bring myself to say
That I love you, or call you step*mom*
Or offer any real terms of endearment
It's not your fault, nor mine

Just the way the cards fell
The Queen of Hearts next to
the Queen of rough Diamonds
Everything in between, just numbers
and mismatched suits

I'm loathed to say it, but you were there
when I needed somebody
And often when I didn't know it
you had a way of seeing through
Sometimes it would catch my breath

You weren't soft. You were the bull
in the shop after the china was broken
Rolling up your sleeves, picking up pieces
not afraid to cut your hands
on the daily daggers I threw

Honestly I don't know why I can't
utter sincere thanks, if only served on ice
with a slice of embittered gratitude
I owe you that much I'm sure
But it's just not where my loyalties lie

Road Kill #3

We sat in the car one day when I was a kid,
the two of us in a rare and treasured moment, and you told me
that you would never marry again. And I believed you
when you said that you still loved her and always would.

I was soothed by the notion that she'd been your forever girl,
that your place as man and wife would always protect our past
from your present, now cradled in another woman's arms.

When wedding bells had sounded for me, and
you'd met my gaze as I descended in ivory, clutching a sea-holly bouquet,
your own announcement came. She broke the news because you
had never been very good at finding the right words for me.

So I dressed her hair, painted her face, tried to make it fit
and I smiled compliantly from the back of the wedding album.
A shawl of broken promises keeping the chill from my shoulders.

VOLUME 4
CANTATA OF SELF COMPOSURE

stuff of dreams

I had a dream last night
that the lump in my throat
was washed away with
a quart of camomile tea
poured into a mouth (now open)
then dispersed like dandelion seeds
an unfamiliar flutter at first
that turned to a steady stream
of words I'd always owned
but never before released

Part 1: Conflicted Resolution

It would be easy to brand you
with my red hot poker thoughts
and distorted dreams of who you were
who you might have been to me
what you did and how the scars
still fester, putrid underneath a treacle glaze

It would be easy to wear your faults
around my neck, the bones and teeth
trinkets of your victories against my loss
teasing at my throat with sharp edges
that don't quite pierce my thin skin, but
cause blisters to form under your thumbprints

Part 2: Conflicted Resolution

It would be easier to cool the searing
twisted metal with a lingering kiss
toss my dark nights to the dream catcher
dress old wounds with salve and flannel
sprinkle patchouli scented petals
on fresh earth and wait for new blooms

It would be easier to trade calcified pieces
for topaz and amethyst droppers which
dangle from ears that strain for new sounds
to surrender my throat in return for your heart
paint over the impressions with a loyal hand
forgive them father for they know not what they do

Along Came You

Our first glance was more of a cliché
than I might have expected.
But that's how it is in matters of true romance.
Eyes met across a crowded room,
you knew the rest you said, but I didn't.
Not then, not in the music or the lights that night.

Didn't see our first son's hair in the flick of yours.
Noticed your eyes, but didn't know how often
they'd look back at me from a brood of tiny faces.
That your first words would echo from the mouths of our babes.
Couldn't see your sparkle light up their smiles, your smile.

How could I have known of our highs and lows?
And there have been lows, and leaps of faith,
and life in between, come to test us, no easy ride,
but inside those arms of yours I come undone, always have.

I was lost to the night, hidden in dark corners.
Then along came you, a light hidden under a bushel
always there, though you never tried to outshine.
Something I thank the heavens and more for.

From boy to man, evolving through your endeavors.
You think I don't remember the past, the songs of our heart.
I do. Not like you, but it means so much to know
that you hold on to moments I let slip through your safety net.
You, the key holder for our hopes and dreams,
my fears, our tears, and tantrums. Our best and my worst.

And I hope and trust that you won't walk away,
unlock the past and watch me free fall into the black.
No coming back. Empty space without you and
that first glance, which was no more of a cliché
than our happy ever after.

Never Enough for Loving

Unable to conceive that there was enough
In me for you to find, without
pushing past the scum ring
to reach the porcelain underneath

I would peck at your eyes so you could see
the pit
of my empty stomach,
so hungry for crumbs and seed
No amount of which
would swell enough to satisfy
my appetite
for affirmations

All the while you sat as silent witness
As I tried to catch your thoughts
of being too good for me

But your mind did not wander
Your eyes stayed fixed on mine
And for the longest time I
kept
on
kicking

My tantrums testing the boundaries
of your tolerance zone

There was a time I forced
Your face
To
Falter
at my hands

A sharp intake of breath
Fell stale at my feet
And I
Was frozen
On a cold shelf of *what have I done?*

A patient angel must have
Brought you back to me
I'm not sure I deserved you
But there you were

And here we are still
You and I
Angel eyes covered now and then
And faces falter again
While we navigate
Our way back
to a waxing moon

Nobody Told Me How

I don't know how to be here
Nobody told me how to behave
Or what makes a mother immune
To the newborn cries that
Drift into the air, twisting into
The hypnotic columns of the sitar
The wire pick flicking at my raw nerves

The shock and awe tactics
Deployed by the onset of hard labours
Are lost love to a war widow
Every surge bringing me closer to a son
I don't yet know, have not seen or felt
But further from any chance to go back
And ask for help, to be a babe in arms again

I didn't believe it when they told me you were born
Didn't want to, for with you came calling
A master of ceremonies and I was bereft of protocol
So I waved you away, tuned in to my tenderness so sore
And you found your father's arms while I lay numb
Searching for lost love in my anaesthesia

To This Day

I breathe a thousand butterflies
When I hear you turn the key
Still carve your name with arrow point
As I sit beneath the tree, of magnolia
You planted for a child that never was
And when I'm pressed beneath you
I lie trembled there because
There's a safety on your shoulder
I keep cradled to my breast
Where traded for a thousand tears
You laid me down to rest

Insomnia

I'm a mother now but there are nights when I revert to that child. Black nights drawing long shadows that threaten me as tiny sounds punctuate the silence, ringing in my ears like a claxon call. Adrenaline rushes force body trembles that jerk my listless legs with sharp uncoordinated motion, and my mouth is dry.

You lie next to me in sleeping sighs heavy and deep. I reach for your hand and your tired eyes search for my face in the darkness, but before I can find the words you are lost, sucked in by the exhaustion of another day. The nights have never been a safe place to stay, no time for being rested and vulnerable because that's when the bogeyman likes to call without taking shape or form, just taunting as I lie. I splutter through a deafening scream yet I know that only tremulous sounds leave my lips unheard, and your strong features anchor me for a second, your face gently crumples on one side as you press it to the pillow.

I self-soothe with a turn to a familiar rendezvous, an attempt to satisfy a need that can never be met. I've been coming to this place ever since I was a girl, not every night, but many nights since she left. The sunshine in this imaginary place splits the night to make way for my self-constructed sanctuary. Warming my face with amber and gentle breeze as I step through the break in the dense hedges.

I sit and wait under the decorated branches of the solitary cherry tree, its long blossom-covered limbs reaching out to cradle me. My bare feet wriggle in the soft grass, green blades poke tiny gaps between my toes. My gaze shifts only for the aerial display of petals that fall in swirls from the branches. I work my thumb and forefinger along the broderie anglaise frill on my dress, back and forth, finding every tiny hole in the lacy needlework. My hair is as it always was, soft curls entwined into a plait, I know she likes it that way, though it's been twenty years since she last ran my hair through her hands and told me so.

A slideshow of memories runs through my mind, moving me to lie on the grass and curl myself like a newborn. The side of my face prickles as it touches down on the dewy ground and I imagine it to be her touch, her smile and rhythmic heart. Sometimes I think I might like to stay here forever, sometimes I struggle to be the woman I now am and in a moment the endorphins chase the adrenalin, calming my tremble as they trickle in like opiates off the back of a fire hot spoon.

My hunger finally satiated I separate slowly, taking care not to break the connection too soon as I turn my back to the cherry tree, move away from the soft sun and drift quietly back toward the night. I feel her trailing closely behind; her unseen hand slipped into mine for just a moment, and then it is gone. I don't turn to look back, choosing instead to hold on to this feeling as I roll beneath the duvet and lean into you in a softer state at last.

And I am, for tonight I am restored. I am the abandoned child found. By morning our daughter will call out for us and I will go to her. Place her childish hand in mine and whisper into her eager ear, *Sometimes only a mother will do, darling girl,* as we sway in cradle hold.

Racing to Keep Up With Myself

Perhaps your self-made-man status
inspired my thirst for more
Or the speed of life and death
pushed me forward at a pace
The family script, be your best

My fated soul, I predicted so often
might burn before taking root
Just like hers did, and so
no time to waste, so much to do
Rushing on like White Rabbit
in Alice's wonderland
Don't let me be too late
my clock is ticking
Surely I will run out of time
It has happened before
it is all I know to be true
My eyes don't see other possibilities
So I keep my head down and drive
forward to who-knows-where

No time to stop and map my route
Just make my mark, so I might
craft new heirlooms for my passing
Footprints and finger prints
laid in stone and sand
For one day in the future I presume
I won't be there, I can't see past
your thirty-six years or mine

But I will not resign, not yet
Not until I create something
worth leaving behind in my name
in her name, in our name
So back to work,
just a girl racing to keep up

Three Wishes

Your weathered skin still surrounds a bright smile and
those twinkling eyes that have stood the test of time
shining through the battles and blows to your brow
and *I wish* it could have been different, that my need
to rinse out my heart hadn't sucked you down the plughole
with every memory emptied onto pages with my pocket change

But you see, I thought I'd tried to put you first and protect
your kindness from my weaknesses, sponge the stains
from the crisp white spaces that stretched between us
because I love you and my loyalties lie wherever you are
I wish I hadn't absorbed mistakes we made as you caught
the hot potato of circumstance in your calloused hands

If they'd given us the guidebook, compass, and a map
we might have found our way through the thickets and thorns
that cut us all to ribbons in one way or another I'm sure
I wish that we'd been gifted with a tonic for the torture
so that today could be set free of stories
and I'm sorry that I felt the need to find my remedy here

Measuring Up to You

I'd raised you up so high, too high maybe
Perched atop my shrine of memories
Crafted from old photos and your locket

Some images were built on facts
Though it's possible some others
Were soft focus and rinsed in Vaseline

There's no doubt you were one special lady
I knew it would take some sharp tailoring
A nip and tuck if I were to measure up

Nobody ever ordered it explicitly
It was just frequently implied and I knew
Our similarities outnumbered our differences

Same hair, same eyes, same crooked smile
Creativity running through us like a river
Our bodies moulded from matching landscapes

Our stories connected, though the sentences now broken
As I grew, you melted into me and I became you
Until I wondered if I'd ever been anyone else

With the joy of remembering you
Through all our similarities, came the fear
That your fate was mine, no air to call my own

So I would be forced to gasp for breath
A dwindling star amongst the diamonds, just like you
And all the other icons (for only the good die young)

At times I would imagine the perks (there are some)
Not getting old and ragged, remembered at my best
No time to get stale, no witnesses to my decline

Every day I'd feel for a lump, half hoping I'd find one
So I could give in and deliver my swansong
Much easier than sitting in the reeds waiting to be found

Time keeps rolling on and now I'm at the age you were then
And I realise I have existed longer without you
Than the years of magical moments spent held in your arms

And I don't remember why you still define me
Everything I am, everything I am not
Time has made us strangers, forced me into a new day

The day when I finally began to hold on to me
By letting go of you, fingertip by fingertip
So I could turn the page and write my own story

Years in the Making

I've waited for this time to come
heavily pregnant with the anticipation
adrenalin has curdled my blood
for the twenty-five years in the making of this day

I've hidden behind the curtain call
unable to face the inevitability of my encore
my time to carve a new future
in the chipped bark of our family tree

I've found my voice amongst the stutters
felt for possibilities lying at the bottom
of the velvet bag of playing cards
I'm ready to take my turn, and deal

Back to the Centre

Hello to the little girl at the centre.
I left you behind all of those years ago
and now I see you there, smiling,
hiding in your fantasy land
of princesses and ballerinas,
handsome princes come to rescue
your songs and rainbows,
drawings and colour, lots of colour.

As the years have passed
I have wrapped layer upon layer
around you, carefully preserving,
leaving you there, mummified,
frozen in time. I meant to
come back, I long to still,
but where to restart,
unearth that old life, and so
I wait to see your innocent
eyes open again,
awakened from your dark sleep
to continue the journey.

Pick up all the colours of the rainbow,
sing every note strong and loud,
draw your memories,
and breathe again,
keep those gifts safe for me
because I'm coming back to you
soon . . .

I'll hold your hand in mine, entwined
as we mark our trail through
an enchanted forest of futures untold,
there are still so many places for us to go.

~

Gratitude

With thanks to Kellie Elmore for giving me the inspiration to start even if you didn't know it. Natasha Head, Stuart McPherson, Louise Hastings, and Bobbie Ward, your incredible talents combined with your kind words and encouragement have made me a better poet.

About the Author

Vanessa Matthews began her creative journey as a child, finding her voice through writing after losing her mother at a very early age. This tragedy sent Vanessa down a path of self-discovery which ultimately led to *Melodies of My Other Life*, a poetry collection that documents a happy childhood unexpectedly impacted by loss, grief, rebellion, dysfunction, and a search for resolution. With words that touch hearts, stir emotions, and create lasting images, Vanessa successfully places her readers directly into her journey. In addition to her poetry, Vanessa is a keen fiction writer and blogger, and is currently working on a full-length novel from her home near the coast in the county of Cornwall, England.

Follow Vanessa
Website: ordinarylifelessordinary.wordpress.com
Twitter: twitter.com/VanessaMatthews
Facebook: facebook.com/VanessaMatthewsWriter